Return of the Orb Weaver

poems by

Michael D. Jones

Finishing Line Press
Georgetown, Kentucky

Return of the Orb Weaver

Copyright © 2020 by Michael D. Jones
ISBN 978-1-64662-140-8 First Edition
All rights reserved under International and Pan-American Copyright Conventions. No part of this book may be reproduced in any manner whatsoever without written permission from the publisher, except in the case of brief quotations embodied in critical articles and reviews.

ACKNOWLEDGMENTS

Crosswinds Poetry Journal, Spring 2018, Letting Go, or The Dead Ask Again
80 Trips Around The Sun, Summer 2017, Reflecting on The Waters of Life
Passion Pages, Spring 2017, Surprise 20th Anniversary Party
1st Prize, Muskegon Museum of *Art Ekphrastic* Poetry Competition 2018 (April), Sponsored by the Poetry Society of Michigan, Standing on the First Tee with His Urn

Publisher: Leah Maines
Editor: Christen Kincaid
Cover Art: stijnpeters, Pixabay
Author Photo: Tina Klein, Klein Photography
Cover Design: Elizabeth Maines McCleavy

Printed in the USA on acid-free paper.
Order online: www.finishinglinepress.com
        also available on amazon.com

        Author inquiries and mail orders:
              Finishing Line Press
                P. O. Box 1626
          Georgetown, Kentucky 40324
                   U. S. A.

Table of Contents

Preparing to Entertain Someone's Somebody 1
Sparrows Without a Nest 2
Google Maps Girl 3
I Am Trying to Write This Poem 4
What The Breeze Carries 5
Anticipating the Carey Cup 6
Standing on the First Tee with His Urn 7
Driftwood Fire 8
Ode for Tillermen 11
Suspecting the Bathroom Fan 12
Hornets' Nest in Fall 13
Anatomy of a Grass Whistle 14
Always The Wind 15
Of Clouds and Smoke 16
The Blessing of Ticks 17
Winter Mornings Listening 18
To The Anonymous Gentleman 21
Landscaping Conifers 22
Little Messengers 23
Reflecting on The Waters of Life 24
Noticing a Change in Her Penmanship Only 25
Letting Go, or The Dead Ask Again 26
Sweet Complexities 27
Hoarder Mouse in Bronze Relief 31
Return of the Orb Weaver 32
Surprise 20th Anniversary Party 33
Cleaning Out Wequetonsing 34
Spring Thunder 35
Tonight I Will Sit Out 36

Preparing to Entertain Someone's Somebody

The family oriental by the front door
First impressions and all, and other such

Niceties; the oil painting of the water
Carrier, the pumpkin spice candles lit
Without the customary tea cup plates

Fine ten and twelve-year holiday Scotch
Once or twice a year stuff, not too much

Though. I need to vacuum the bamboo
Again, and maybe plant some flowers.

I too am someone's somebody who makes
An artful fuss in their special way: attention
To detail, to other; the preparation is all.

Blinds can remain open, depending on
Daylight; slant may vary accordingly.

Sparrows Without A Nest

November rain with forecasted snow and
here I marvel at my summer spider, still
clinging since May to the window frame
it has turned since yesterday evening, faces
away from the front door with eight eyes
some of which admire the bright red leaves
of our Japanese Maple, most fully alive
gasping brilliance in this bleak landscape
of bare poplars and elms, cold and wet.
I failed to notice the small red breasted
sparrows, two of them, until I turned off
the porch light and they flit, flew and lit
settling under the eave; one facing me
one ever vigilant, the spider between us.
I wonder if they see me, see the fat spider
if they remember May or even have a nest.

Google Maps Girl

Some say she speaks in tongues
weaving what-ifs and hard facts.
She neither sings nor croons.
Then I take a left too soon, miss
my anticipated exit, am delayed
by an accident I can't even see
while others slowly roll past
and her tongue promises another
smooth path, another fastest route
to my destination. I place some faith
in her assurances. I will get there
eventually; such is my experience.
I am prone to also follow clouds
interpreting their shape and shift
and sometimes simply feeling
my way across town, crawling
down empty streets, my car
windows down inviting sounds
the squeals of children at play
the bark of dogs, occasional
sirens, and her saying *right right
right,* even though it oddly sounds
more like a question than the truth.
Often, I will make small mistakes
just to hear her voice recalculate.
Her intentions are for my best.

I Am Trying to Write This Poem

Have you seen my hat and gloves?
She asks the coat tree outside my office.
I am trying to write. If they go
to the second bridge, it could happen
the poem if not the poetry, or
if it is just around the block I'm screwed.
The good news is they pooped

both dogs (I'm informed); I notice
their too happy *we-pooped-in-snow* dance
burst through my office door
both distraction and inspiration. Perhaps
"The Cat", after Galway Kinnell. No.
I am trying to write this poem now.
Colleen needs time at the library

worries about breaking the frame
about returning home for lunch, and
I hear Amy did a bunch of chores
it's just she and Jim, she and Jim, then
something about Maria and blankets
washes over my head like winter air.
I sang, *They're on the hallway chair.*

What the Breeze Carries

The first time you were much younger
and in love with all the many things
the young are forever in love with
open windows, what the breeze carries
lilacs on the air, pre-dawn bird song
the wafting drip and gasp of creation
coffee brewed in another room
soft autumn air, the murmur of leafy trees
the murmur of blinking lights in trees
like stars, and stars themselves twinkling
distant and cold and forever fixed
the sting of snow while waiting to cross
a half-lit city street, the surging crowd
all the rhythms of diner spoons and cups
and voicemails saved; their love-
missives replayed on darker days.
I too so loved these many things
and reading of your bougainvillea's
geraniums, toads, the curve of a spine
breath of horses; vapor under pressure
stardust, grains dilating across the pages
once more recognizably of their time.

Anticipating the Carey Cup, June 2017
For Tim Carey, In Abstentia

Defending Carey Cup champion Patrick Carey
who past champion Ron Lang conferred said title
Ron, who years ago witnessed The Hole-in-One
heard-'round-the-world with Ed Kieser, Michael
Carey's brother-in-law and Brother Rice alum
along with Chris Carey who now orchestrates
in Memoriam of their father, Michael Carey
and now the late Dennis DeClerk, who grilled
the steaks into perfection while Sherman recites
our favorite monologue from A Few Good Men
every year; *The Truth: The Truth. You can't
handle the Truth.* The Carey's children's children
will read these names inscribed along with years
year after year and hear the tales of golfers past.

Standing on the First Tee with His Urn

The box open, exposing his flecks of bone
Fine ash sifted in a plastic bag
We each chose to dip our tender hands in

After the funeral luncheon, on the first tee
Sniffing winter's first green of spring
Before the curious golfers emerge, their shadows

Just beginning to form in half-light; the new
Season of desire where we remain
And breathe this raw freedom, cold and sharp

The death of our father and part of ourselves
Owning his small betrayals, occasional
Fairway apples, and now this box of ashes.

Driftwood Fire

Wood that drifts, water-worn
Stone smooth tree trunks and limbs
river debris from logging camps

flotsam of shipwrecks, the carnage
of broken homes swept out to sea
by hurricanes and Tsunami tides

how far you have come to shelter
the dune grass, orb weavers, crabs
how your decay feeds the shore

your over-worked, tide-twisted
sun-soaked, and worm-riddled
sculpted bodies our natural profit

the stuff of eco-art and lakeshore
décor; you as wall clock, windmill
Trojan horse, Tipi, ghost ship.

***

You make a curious fire.
You often pop, emitting orange cinders.
You burn low and slow.

You think you are water.
Your free radicals are blue-green.
The EPA warns of toxins.

***

*...I had a bad case of driftwood
and forgot to tuck it when I went
to work. -Urban Dictionary*

Euphemisms abound for driftwood.
The culture and slang of driftwood
travels fast; not far from its source.

An older guy that drifts around.
A solitary individual who aimlessly
bounces around on the dance floor

engaging in unwanted advances.
A random ____; stiffy from _____.
Wood that never finds its port. (ibid)

***

There would be giant sea monsters, and I
would be a survivor
                          an empty sherry cask
then a lonely lone stave of hardened oak

a saturated rib from a seasoned oak cask
a sea floor stave
                          of a sunken survivor
a tisket, a tasket,
            a broken sherry cask   et

awash in the wash
                        current in the current
whittled and wattled
                        fiddled and faddled
a scuttling sea paddle
                        tussled and tasseled

bobbing and weaving
                        coming and leaving
sifting, shifting,   drifting
burning slowly with
                        toxins; intoxicating.

***

Fear is reasonable; the fire burns.
This primal fascination, however

is another thing; how we huddle
close/not too close, our inner heat

radiant and familiar in the night
flickering like stars or open flames

their orange tongue licking along
near exhausted bones of driftwood

a reminder that we too are part light
part whatever else escapes the night

as if the fires of ardor burn eternal
in a universe where everything fades

or is transformed; reborn otherwise
broken, scattered, and re-imagined.

Tonight, on this porch of shoreline
driftwood fires pop and glow, emit

tiny sparks also, twinkling like stars
their reflections float on waves.

Ode for Tillermen

Favorable winds
on open seas seldom find
rudderless sailboats.

Suspecting the Bathroom Fan

I am beginning to suspect the bathroom fan
in our back-hall laundry area, with
the bonus half-bath, is involved. Of course
I can only speculate at this point as
there is a lunar eclipse next week which implies
the potential for all types of odd behaviors
(if not retinal damage), and I could miss seeing
a clue as to why our new Maytag electric dryer
has suffered a PF twice in the past two days
leaving our clothes still damp and forlorn.
Or it could be Karma, a word I don't often use
but which appeared with increasing regularity
this past week like magic; or misdirection as
electricity, bathroom fans, and laundry dryers
are relatively recent advancements and new
technology seems immune to past-life experience.
Anyhow, I suspect the laundry bathroom fan.
My electric clippers and Joanne's blow dryer
or even the vacuum in our bedroom will
blow a circuit on the main panel if
our bathroom fan is on at the same time.
This could explain the motherboard going
last month on the old Whirlpool Sport Elite.
Magic, or Karma, or coincidence I think not
although they are on two different circuits.
Perhaps it is foreshadowing and the foreknown
(Power Failure; Power Failure; Lunar Eclipse).
That and not to look directly: never directly.

Hornets' Nest in Fall

Before they go dormant in October, hornets
nest beneath our gable like a grey paper
lantern, all electric-buzz and spark within

And when did this happen, this stinging life
constructing its globe at the peak of our home?

How long these hot, interminable, summer days
and nights spent gathering, masticating, and
almost religiously netting this thin veil of grey

this hornet's nest with its idiocentric network
roughly the size of my head, with its grey hairs

And rude habit of self-involvement, distraction
of self and (when my prayerful best) selflessness?
Sensing the season's inevitable end, hornets

Like us in our terminal days, increasingly become
agitated in their throws, without reflection sting

Anything within their reach (if not their grasp)
these final days of summer, heat rising off shingles
soft light declining, everything that can preparing.

I'm going to need help with this one; more than
Joanne and the kids, more than a few neighbors.

My head buzzes from unreconciled disparities
like hot hornets gasping late summer heat, those
final moments where words fail and sounds prevail.

Anatomy of a Grass Whistle

A broad green blade of grass
firmly held between two thumbs

from Distal Phalanx to Trapezium
(which is nothing like a group

of people moving together; or
a circus trapeze for two, and nearly

invisible like two trapeze wires
that vibrate and sing when cutting air

as they briskly swing; lips pressed
firmly as if to kiss one's knuckles)

and blow gusty as spring until
the grass too awakens and whistles.

Always the Wind

Excites the ground, ground waters, the grass
Leafy low branches and the tops of trees

Clouds that build and those that thin in sun.
Excites and drives the rain, dead leaves like rain

April showers, flowering buds and budding flowers
The wings of birds and birds that sing on the wind

Monarchs and ragweed, the muffled cries of lovers.
Always the wind. Always the wind. The wind

Lubricates the present, thaws the now of now
Or coldly whips the falling future into snow

Propels the essential kite of experience; words
Like daisies, bumble bees, honey
                              tomorrow: God.

Of Clouds and Smoke

Difficult low clouds
drifting grey beneath

a sky of higher white
cloud deck this evening

as blue smoke rises
from my cigar ash

blue like my longing
for you, my muse, with

leafy green tree limbs
the only horizon, as I

recline into this canvas
lounge chair, discerning

clouds from cloud deck
Love from other loves.

The Blessing of Ticks

The ticks are thick along the path

again this Spring, another mild
winter, another forgiving April

except for hungry ticks that cling
to rabbits, diseased deer, possum

the soft underbellies of our dogs

and would find their way into our
linens and undergarments, our

epidermis, if we did not somehow
touch; inspecting, affirming.

Winter Mornings Listening
for Joanne

(To The Darkness At My Desk While Missing You; Or,
The Physics Of Longing And Loneliness In White: How It Goes
When The Dogs Sleep And You Are Not Around)

January morning winter dark, the monitor
hums, humming, its fan whirring pre-dawn
pre-first line inspiration; pre-ten thirty walk.

One barks at bus stop children, one drinks
water from the water dish. Let's begin where
we are with what we have, a repeated sense

of loss, a desperate longing for the muscular
mind, trees with leaves then fruit, imagined
half-dreamt friends seen briefly on vacation.

Whatever became of our wedding party?
Dalilah dens beneath my desk, on my feet
soon she will move to the front door rug

in anticipation. Webster remains in bed
like a stuffed animal, napping like a baby
silently no longer barking like a dog, he

by virtue of being on the bed, is not a dog.
However, later on our walk we will all know
the cold cleanliness of snow; fresh powder

exposing footprints, all I make without you.

**

morning winter dark, the monitor
hums, humming, its fan whirring
pre-first line inspiration; pre-ten thirty walk.

    barks at bus stop children, one drinks
water from the water dish   where
we are with what we have, a repeated sense

of loss, a desperate   the muscular
mind, trees with leaves then
half-dreamt friends seen   on vacation.

                    wedding   ?
Dalilah dens beneath my desk, on my
soon she will move to the front door

          Webster
   stuffed   napping like a baby
silently no longer barking like a dog, he

               on the bed, is not a dog.
However,   on our walk we will all know
the cold cleanliness of snow;   powder

exposing footprints, all I make without

                 **

January
                    pre-dawn
.

One
              Let's begin

          longing for
              fruit, imagined
        briefly

.
Whatever became of our   party
                               feet
                               rug

    anticipation.   remains
            animal

by virtue of being

                       fresh

                              you.

To The Anonymous Gentleman

At Planet Fitness in Holland last Monday
evening, Thank You
                  for returning my
watch, a gift; the beefy stainless automatic
the sporty one with carbon fiber face and
luminescent hands
                  and matching band.

Learn how to model, Charles Wright schooled
before you learn to finish things.
                          Life imitates
Art, I suppose; the natural and more than that.
I mostly take care of the time I've been given
although imperfect still I
                  seek the golden rule
luminescent; if not stainless, sporty and beefy.

Thank you for doing what I aspire to do if
I ever find my neighbors' watch
                        left behind
in the men's locker room, resting on a shelf
in an otherwise clean locker
                      after 5:00
the seconds silently sweeping past: around
and around, and around; what comes around.

Landscaping Conifers

The thinking goes
                it is green all year long
and when it grows it will be bushy dense
and block the view of the neighbors' cars
in their driveway
                returning home at night.
That's the idea. Yet, I've seen too many
landscaping conifers
                blue spruce, juniper
and evergreen, brittle and bare come spring
their branches
                a totem of tiny crucifixes
as if they too understood right from wrong
and refused to play along
                on principle alone
showing us how we live together, or not.

Little Messengers

Little angels, little envoys
from beyond: a subtle
shift in the wind, little bird
song sent my way
anything unusual in
the night or in flame.
I hear no problems in
the afterlife for you
your accounts are settled
your intercessions, ceded.
Last October, garage crickets
then later snow squalls, rogue
sunshine in winter, nesting
birds this spring in our eaves
the cries of unseen chicks
soon to fledge, now
anything that flies:
bumblebees, cardinals
hummingbirds, dragonflies
and sometimes sunlight.
I listen for your warmth.

Reflecting on the Waters of Life
for Earl Wolfe on his 80th

The last time we drank most
deeply into your best whiskey
and my bottle too, a warming gift
opened in your living room filled
with authors, poems and stories

laughing until we clichéd or cried
(we've all been there), the tears
churning like the Detroit River
in Spring, heavy with gratitude
frothy from snows and driving rain

and also the damp dry of autumn
groves, the crisp air soon mellow
with joyful music from your piano
Diana's favorite, notes like deer
the huntress would dutifully follow

now tracing memory down the years
your fingers nimbly tracking keys
across the rivers and many seasons
once more sharing your dulcet tones
with dear friends that pour and flow.

Noticing a Change in Her Penmanship Only

Her wavering hand stammers to tell me something
Many happy returns of the day, Best Wishes
a check for running shoes, a champagne toast
for the sun also rising; a bubbly Mimosa sun
going down. How her arthritic pain rips a whistle
like steam from the kettle scalds her small bones
her cartilage-free joints. Still, she sings *Happy
Birthday, Son. You've meant a lot to me. Love
You always*
              Mom   The plus-plus of time
obeys a balanced order where we are no longer
love without pain and grow singularly grateful.
Thanks for the toast, the years, the shoes, the tears
humble beginnings, birthdays, the warming sun.
Her knotted hands pressed together in prayer
the rising tide of gratitude bubbles and boils
heat that loosens muscle; bring ice for her joints.

Letting Go, or The Dead Ask Again

Whiskey evenings sorting papers, then
the next month languishes like wax
down the side of candles; dripping beads
re-dripping beads. Nothing could be done
beyond that. Grief's slow turning moves
no faster. Whatever brokenness demands
healing could heal no faster. *Drip. Drip.*

The dead eventually ask to be buried again
and foresee that now is the time of burial
and (unlike any wilted flower that remains
too long) open-up into the universe, change
the weather from candle wax and flicker
to heavy rains and wind advisories. Floods
of energy; invisible streams of resolution.

Fruit flies quit the vineyards and pumpkins
return to their patch. Trees speak leaves
fragile after weeks of pained consideration
calling. Ready, she said at this point even
Tupperware would do. He said something
had to be done, a decision, a blue urn with
inscription; then the soonest date possible.

Light the last candle, bring your finest silk
flowers, pin your grandmother's broach, throw
on your tie and overcoat, consign your haircut
the dead are ready for burial and have asked.
Let the wick exhaust itself, and wax be only
the shell of flame; the flame free of its wick
ready to join all that inhabits the otherness.

Sweet Complexities
i.m. Mary Cay Jones, 1930-2017

1.
Quintessence of sugar, quintessence of dust
Mother of lemon bars dusted with sugar
Brightly tart, unbearably sweet, lemon squares
Of cookies you no longer could make once
Your own Mother passed; Nana, who in her
Final months would forget ingredients: flour
We would tell her after sampling her wares.
Lemon squares would never taste so good again.
How will the sun rise when we forget the flour?
How is it that after a lifetime of enlargements
Everything seemingly reduces to tiny grains
And then nothingness; the invisible beyond?
You were always there before we were; breath
before breath, our first self before ourselves.
Your love is no less now that it lacks breath
So long as we, your legacy, continue to breathe
And persevere in understanding of your ways
With what force your stately world did turn
How like lemon squares your love manifests.

2.
Like flight, every madness has its method.
She would have flags, even if no wind
And ceramic flags if too much wind.
She admired fireworks so much that
She dimmed her porch light not to detract
And cared little for bonfires or sparklers.
Clouds were ice cream, cotton candy, fluff
Heavenly bodies sent for her musing delight
And rain a curse no umbrella could dispel.
Sail boats on spinnaker runs were majestic
Their colored sail cloth billowing the tail wind
Both catching to hold and lift, then spilling.

However, there should be a law against jet skis.
Soap bubbles and confetti; manmade rainbows
With pots of gold no one could ever find.
She joyfully joined her choir's cacophony
Social clubs and charity boards with meetings
And dues, and their selfless obligations.
Emissaries understood she knows the boss
In lieu of God, prayers and Angels would do.

3.
Like parades, every method has its madness.
They end with first responders and police escorts
Begin with honor guards, guns and flags (again)
Followed by more veterans in full military dress
In open cars waving as though they just arrived
High school bands, civic groups with banners
Volunteer firemen, a zillion flowers dotting floats
Faces on crowded bleachers mirroring the street.
Methodical. Orderly. Compartmentalized. Then
Clowns on roller skates, clowns with big heads
Interspersed among the groups, erratic as drunks
They dart and weave surprising the crowd
With candy, super soakers, and confetti cannons.
They are the madness we crave like a fresh breeze
Blowing open our kitchen windows, clearing
The stodgy air, disrupting stacks of papers, webs
And dust, unsettling our plans, disturbing dreams.
Such are forces of nature, so compelling parades
She could only watch them on television, or from
Inside her home as they passed; safe and secure.

4.
Basically, all that was heaviness was in on it.
The burden of possession wanted to possess her
And her accounts would hold her accountable.

Unpacked moving boxes mingled with QVC
Boxes in her foyer, under her desk, on top of her

Library table; boxes shelved on stairs like books.
Summer and fall up-north, winters in Florida
The spring where she came from, memory
Inescapably comforting her like nursery rhymes.
Her homes, newly built or remodeled for her
In her image, at her expense. She held on to
Unopened mail more than seven years old
Files with un-cashed checks, thank you notes
Expired coupons, and legal documents. At eighty
She considered going grey at last; too late
As her children's children would have none.
A bibliophile, her favorite genre was cookbooks.
In her kitchen, where she stopped cooking years ago
Slips of faded newspaper with recipes randomly
Appear like pennies in pant pockets or snow squalls.
She stopped updating her personal account in July
And several entries are missing in her Foundation
Register; fortunately, she kept recognition letters
Some from nearly twenty years ago on her desk.
She decorated with monkeys she could never own.

5.
She quickly took to air travel, and traveled
In flocks and gaggles, in business and first.
Her passport spoke for itself in romance.
Robins sang her spring return, her summer
Season of cocktail parties and luncheons
Her visits with friends, coming and going
And cardinals questioned her migrations.
Bats routinely patrolled for circling pests.
Everything that flew was in on it although
She seemed not to notice the butterflies

That followed her daily, but commented
On foxes and wild turkeys that wandered
Across the lawn. Her hair was the sun
And her eyes the deepest bright blue of sky
Her tiny hands both wanting and giving
As the Carpathian Mountains; and hard

To cross like mountains, unless you fly.
She glided when she walked, as if skating
On concrete. Cobblestone was troublesome.
She celebrated with wines she never drank.

6.
Her business manager up-north, Donna Weber
Particularly admires Mom's paper shredder
It too transforms unneeded things into parades.

Hoarder Mouse in Bronze Relief
After Pack Rat by E.C. Wynne

The mouse must be exhausted
From pine cones and peanut shells
Bottle caps, beads, buttons, light bulbs
Paper clips, pins, spools and string
And here is someone's lucky penny
Stuck on a stick, there a missing key
And an official whistle. Time out.
Her eyes are large, her long tail held in
Small hands, her tiny gesture plaintive
Nil Mea Culpa: I am as God made
Compelled to gather these shiny things
Against the nothingness of otherwise
All this mounded with leaves and dirt
A legacy of industry, if not things.

Return of the Orb Weaver

You are early this year, Orb Weaver
Your wide-cast web dominating again
Our patio door wall; welcome, unwelcome
Guest. You stayed all September last year
Knitting and re-knitting your web. Now
It begins again, yet this time is different;
Colleen leaves for her second year
At College, and mothers die only once
Although with us forever, Orb Weaver.
You seem smaller, or perhaps I am older.

Surprise 20th Anniversary Party, September 1976

Once upon a time might surprise once
like miniature franks wrapped in bacon
or wrapped in crescent roll dough
or helplessly swimming in BBQ sauce
sooner or later it's the expected appetizer.
Surprise pales with familiarity. Yet, we
frequent occasions for Love's expression
knowing that once, just once, a surprise party
is surprising- for everyone; the honoree
the guests, and the hosts (which we were
although not old enough to drive a car)
working the room with hors d'oeuvres
dark as ambush, stealthy as covert operation
as sleight of hand magic; your Best Man
and Maid of Honor, friends from the club
former business associates, pot-luck group
and their invisible spouses materialized
infinitely pleased with cheese and crackers
attempting to cut Surprises' dark tension
with cheap wine and colored toothpicks
and our love, hot like miniature franks.
One of many ways love leaves a strange
desire for Spearmint gum, surprises us all.

Cleaning Out Wequetonsing, September 2016

She held everything against dissolution
like stones, and gathered them
like stones piled neatly on her desk
and on the floor next to her desk
in her desk drawers and in empty corners:
Albion College tuition statement
Paid; Woman Descending Stairs
by Nicola Simbari, Paid; Detroit Bank
and Trust Savings account, Closed
(still these cannot be thrown away).
A thank you note from her friend's
charity, dated financial statements
older than seven years, Birthday cards
some received, some never sent
a separate pile to be thrown away.
Stamps in need of other stamps.
Stacks of note pads, boxes of note cards
markers, pens, mechanical pencils
glue sticks, paper clips, rolls of tape
assorted office supplies still in bags
(all of them, all of them, you name it
with their receipts) get donated to charity.
Everything held in self-importance is
eventually exhausted, filed or shredded
in the accounting. Everything must go.
Next is the kitchen, then the closets, then
the emptiness she filled her life with.

Spring Thunder

Stillness and distant thunder out
over Lake Michigan where
clouds refuse to move onshore

another warm spring day in May
and I figure an hour or two before
the high winds and rain arrive.

I also figure there is a chance of
grandchildren, someday.
What will I tell them of thunder?

Will we hike on warm spring days
before the rains, thunder rolling in
the distance? Will they wonder

as I now wonder, will there be lightning?
Today, I tell them not to fear lightning
how lightning comes from heaven

and how lightning brought us here.

Tonight I Will Sit Out

Again, and marvel at the moon
that bright rock in the sky
and allow myself the luxury
of indulging my awe
at the commonplace of night.

Mostly I catch glimpses, slivers
to or from wherever, as I drive
and often at dusk or dawn
take note of the luminous distant
specks shining just above the horizon
and ask Google: What visible planets
can I see today? On a good day
I will call a friend and say, *Look
the moon is so beautiful.*

Is that Mars ascending? Look.
Then countless miles later, *Bye now.*
This never gets old, unlike us
whose unsteady days softly are
measured by what goes around.